HANi

Bless

I AM GRATEFUL TUN
OUR FRIENDSHP & YOUR
LOVE & SUPPORT! with love,

Sacred Keys and Codes to Activate Your Higher Purpose

Cody W. Cooper

ISBN: **1979740046**
ISBN-13: **978-1979740043**

DEDICATION

I dedicate this book to all the beautiful souls who are accepting their divine missions and allowing themselves to step forward on their path of self-mastery and enlightenment. May this book bring divine inspiration, hope, clarity, and purpose to your life, in a spiritually uplifting way, bestowing many blessings upon your life and your soul purpose here on Earth.

For future reference, I use the term God, our Creator, Higher Power, the Divine, the universe, and so on to describe God throughout this book. Please allow yourself to use whatever word resonates with you and your spiritual path. Sometimes one word resonates more than the other, so I allow myself to write the word that wants to come through.

Before beginning chapter 1, it may be helpful for

you to skip ahead and read Chapter 10: Terminology.
This will provide you with clarity on the terminology
that I reference frequently throughout this book.

Also, please reference my book, *Therapy for the
Soul*, for a guided meditation to connect with your
Higher Self as this is referred to often in this book.

CONTENTS

ACKNOWLEDGMENTS

I want to thank the Angelic Realms and my spiritual support team for giving me the inspiration, keys, codes, and activations to bring this book into existence. I am grateful to be deepening my connection to All That Is, while bringing a deeper sense of clarity, guidance, joy, and unconditional love to all.

I want to thank my dad for inspiring me from the higher realms, and thank my family for being so supportive of my work here on Earth. I acknowledge everyone who will read this book and give thanks for all of your love and support. Thank you for allowing me to relay these sacred messages with you in this time of expansion and growth as part of my soul purpose work. May you all be touched deeply with the love emanating from the pages of this book.

CHAPTER 1: DIVINE INTERVENTION

As I read this paragraph, I give myself permission to receive all dispensations of light being offered to me at this time from our Supreme Creator. I allow myself to download and integrate these sacred energetic keys, codes, and energetic frequencies from my Higher Self and the Christ Consciousness energy now. I am fully aware that these activations and light codes are a part of my soul purpose and higher calling, and I gladly accept this energy. In doing so, I know that I AM aligning more fully with who I AM on a soul level, deepening my connection to All That Is. I AM grateful for the divine intervention occurring in my life and I gladly accept wonderful and blissful changes into my life. I give my Angelic Helpers and spiritual support team full permission to help me in all areas of my life. I give thanks for all of the blessings that are about to happen in my life. I am ready. I am ready. I am ready. Through the power of grace and gratitude, Amen!

Though this prayer is simple, don't underestimate its strength. I am proud of each and every one of you who picked up this book, because it means that you listened to your intuition and divine guidance correctly. Pat yourself on the back, because that is an accomplishment in itself! Many times we don't even realize that we are following divine guidance. For instance, we may choose to go to the store to grab shampoo one evening without being consciously aware that we are about to meet someone who says just the right thing at *exactly* the time you needed to hear it. Or you may decide to drive a different way home from work one day, only to find that you see a sign that says "everything is going to be okay" with a picture of a cardinal on it. What may seem like little signs, can actually hold tremendous power. By noticing these signs, you have successfully tuned into your Angelic support team and followed their gentle nudges which let you know that you are on track, and that you are exactly where you need to be at exactly the right time. You receive the clarity, inspiration and encouragement that helps propel you forward at any given moment. More often than not, we will begin to realize that we have been listening to our inner voice and we have been acting upon our Angelic guidance whether we are conscious of it or not. As we do so, the synchronicities keep coming and the messages get more clear. Little did we know that going to grab shampoo or driving a different way home from work was actually a door of opportunity for you to deepen your connection to not only yourself, but to your Angelic team as well!

The main message here is not to force things to happen. Give yourself permission to receive Angelic support in all areas of your life. Then let go and be open to receiving help in unexpected ways. Some of the help given to you may be direct and loud, while other messages may be more subtle. You may realize at a later date that the information or scenarios that you were in were actually part of divine unfoldment to help lead you on your path, answer your prayers, and bring in greater understanding. Always know that the Angels want to be there for you, they want to see you succeed in all that you do and they want to make sure that you learn what you came here to learn. They are here to assist you with your soul's expansion, helping you to discover your own innate divine nature. Therefore, they are going to help you in the best way they see fit. Trust them, they know what they are doing.

Inviting in your Angelic support:

1. I, (state your name), now invite my Angelic helpers and spiritual support team to help me in every area of my life. I now ask for your miraculous divine intervention in my life, to help bring more clarity, understanding, and guidance to me as I fully embrace my soul purpose here on Earth. Amen!

2. Let go and know that you have taken a step in

the right direction just by reading this chapter and repeating the simple prayers provided with divine intent.

3. Allow yourself to now pause and reflect on the material you just read. I highly recommend getting out a journal and dedicating it to this book, as there will be various opportunities for you to journal and reflect throughout the following chapters.

4. Once you have your journal, I encourage you to do this simple meditation.

5. Call upon Archangel Raphael, to surround you in his emerald green cloak of healing energy.

6. Begin taking deep breaths, imagining a ball of golden energy 6 inches above your head and another golden ball 6 inches below your feet.

7. Allow the gold and emerald flame to enfold

your entire being, helping to integrate and activate the sacred keys, codes, and light frequencies you have received.

8. Notice what you feel.

9. Notice what you see.

10. Notice what you hear.

11. Ask if there is any specific message that you need to hear at this time.

12. When ready, allow yourself to wiggle your fingers and toes, and begin rubbing your hands together.

13. Place your hands over your eyes, noticing the beautiful heat emanating from your hands.

14. State "I AM at peace" 3 times in your head. When you feel ready, remove your hands and open your eyes.

15. Write down any immediate thoughts, feelings,

colors, and symbols that you received during this meditation and throughout reading this chapter. Do not judge, just allow yourself to write freely. Write down anything that pops into your head, knowing ALL IS WELL.

16. An important note- you are downloading lots of information in a short period of time. You may receive clarity and information throughout your day today and throughout the rest of the week. This may be presented to you in your physical reality, in your dream state, or both. Again, your Angels and your Higher Self are going to be relaying information to you in ways that are most comfortable and comprehendible to your individual needs. Therefore, starting a dream journal to record your dreams is recommended as well.

17. This is high level work, so I recommend waiting to continue on to the next chapter until tomorrow.

18. Blessings to you all! Thank you Angels!

CHAPTER 2: IDENTIFYING YOUR GIFTS

Everyone receives information from their Angelic support team in different ways. There are hundreds of different ways that we may process, detect, and decode information that we are receiving from Spirit, and it varies from person to person. So, can anyone be psychic? Can anyone be intuitive? I have gone back and forth about this throughout the work that I do, but the answer that really resonated with me came to me while my mother and I were attending a presentation by well known "Hollywood

Medium", Tyler Henry. He was asked this question, and his response was simple. He said, "Think of basketball players, some people are really good at playing basketball and others not so much. What I am trying to say is, yes, everyone can tap into their psychic abilities, but some people are more naturally inclined to these gifts and abilities." That seemed to stick with me and I choose to believe that statement. Through my own personal work and spiritual studies, I have learned that there are many ways that people can work on developing greater intuition and I believe that part of my purpose here is to help others open up their energetic and psychic channels, to help them better connect with their divine gifts and abilities, whatever that may mean for them. I have also learned, through past life regression work and Akashic Record training, that it is part of my purpose

11

to help people reclaim their gifts and abilities from previous lifetimes, by bringing their gifts forward into their current timelines, to help assist them with their soul mission work here on Earth. This means that many have agreed to bring their gifts forward, and reclaim their soul's strength and power, which can be done naturally and quite simply when their soul is ready to receive this. Divine timing is always at play and I tend to attract the right people to me at exactly the right time, to work with Spirit, to help bring about positive change and growth on ones sacred spiritual journey.

During our sessions, we work on clearing out old, outworn energies and patterns, allowing deep healing to occur on a soul level, which in turn, allows healing to take place and progression on their spiritual path to begin and accelerate forward. I work with the client's Higher Self, the Angels, Archangels, and Master Beings of Light to bring forward messages and healing frequencies that can help others at any given moment, always helping them align more fully with their divine life blueprint. I see people from all walks of life and at different stages of their journey, and it is a beautiful process. It is my hope that I may bring greater joy, peace, unconditional love, and divine inspiration into each and every person who comes into my life. That is my truth and that is part of my purpose here on Earth. The journey of the soul is truly sacred.

When aligning more fully with your spiritual nature, you may notice different spiritual gifts "reawakening" or coming into play in your life. We call these extrasensory abilities your "clair" abilities. Below, I will describe some of the major "clair" abilities and ways of identifying the divine guidance that is trying to come through.

1. **Clairvoyance**- This is the gift of spiritual vision. When you are clairvoyant, you are seeing with your spiritual eye, located in your third eye chakra on your forehead. You may see visuals, such as symbols, numbers, sacred geometry, or play-by-play actions as seen while watching a movie screen. You may see this with your eyes open or eyes closed. Clairvoyance is also the ability to receive information in your dream state that may have significance and can help you make informed decisions in your present life. Clairvoyants may see various colors and also report seeing the energy and specific colors of one's energetic field and aura.

2. **Clairaudience**- The gift of clear hearing. People with this gift tend to receive messages through songs and music, hearing exactly the right phrase or message at exactly the right time. They may hear internally or externally. Clairaudient people tend to resonate with sound and vibrations, and will often times report hearing an inner voice that is guiding them. One sign that you are starting to tap into your clairaudient abilities is when you start to hear someone calling your name while in public, only to see that there is no one there. Angels do this to get your attention, and to help you know that you have this gift and are ready to bring it forward more fully into your life. The message they are trying to convey when this

happens is, "tune in". Set some time aside to connect with your spiritual support team and ask your Guardian Angels to help you hear their loving guidance and reassurance. Like anything, it gets easier with practice.

3. **Clairsentience**- The gift of clear feeling. This gift is complex and takes a little while to get used to. People who are clairsentient, feel the energetic transfers of energy in people, places, and things. This is a common gift among empathetic people, as they have a heightened sensitivity to the energy of others and their environments. When honed appropriately and understood, this is a powerful tool that can make a huge difference on a global level. Clairsentient people are able to take this gift one step

further, and learn to transmute the energy around them to a higher frequency and have the potential to be tremendous healers in this world. If you find yourself to be clairsentient, you may benefit from taking a reiki course or healing touch class to learn more about how you can use your gifts to serve on a greater level.

4. **Claircognizance**- The gift of clear knowing. This gift is one of the most valuable gifts, in my opinion. Claircognizant people tend to "just know" information without any apparent reason. I believe this is because they are able to process higher energetic information instantaneously. As you raise your vibrational frequency and let go and let God, you start to become a more pure and

clear conduit for spiritual energy and are able to hold a great quotient of spiritual light. Therefore, the information that you "just know" resonates with you on a soul level, often times presenting itself with electrical jolts of energy, known as "spiritual goosebumps". I find that this reassurance will help you overcome all doubt and worry of being judged, giving you the reassurance you need to relay specific information with ease and grace. I believe that the information that becomes available to you is a direct message from your Angelic team of light.

Exercise to awaken your spiritual channels of light:

1. Find a place where you can relax and be undisturbed.

2. Light a white candle and dedicate it to the

Holy Spirit and your Angelic team of light.

3. Ground yourself by visualizing a golden chord moving down from your heart center, through your solar plexus, navel, sacral, base, and earth star chakras. Allow this golden chord to connect to the heart of Mother Earth, which you will see as a giant bubble of pure luminescent pink energy, located in the center of the Earth.

4. Connect with this pink energy and allow that relaxing energy to come up through your ankles, knees, hips, heart center, shoulders, neck, and through the crown of your head. Allow the energy to bathe you in a beautiful, relaxing energy that soothes your body, mind, and spirit.

5. Now imagine a pure, white ball of energy

from the Holy Spirit surrounding your entire physical body.

6. Call in your Higher Self to join you.

7. Allow yourself to center your attention and awareness in your heart center and give yourself permission to stay centered in your heart throughout this sacred transmission of light. Allow all distractions and worry to be transmuted by the sacred flame, allowing a deep sense of peace and stillness to wash over you now.

8. Give yourself permission to connect more deeply with your Angelic support team and Higher Self now. Notice any colors, symbols, words, objects, and messages you receive at this time.

9. Now through divine will and divine intent,

repeat the following: "I, (state your name), now choose to fully light up and activate my clairvoyant abilities to a level that is appropriate for me at this time. Awaken, awaken, awaken!"

10. Take a moment and observe what this looks like and how this feels.

11. Then repeat, "I now choose to fully light up and activate my clairaudient abilities in a way that is perfect for me at this time, through the power of divine grace, amen! Activate, activate, activate!"

12. Take a moment and notice what you notice.

13. Then repeat, "I now fully light up and activate my clairsentient abilities through the power of God's Divine will. Amen! Activate, activate, activate!"

14. Notice the thoughts and feelings that come about as you continue these powerful invocations of light.

15. Next, repeat, "I now choose to fully light up and activate my claircognizant gifts and abilities, to help me with my "inner knowing" and Angelic connection, through the power of grace and the power of gratitude. Amen! Activate, activate, activate!"

16. Take a moment to notice the powerful energy that you just received and the energy that is surrounding you at this time.

17. Allow yourself to lock in these frequencies by asking your Higher Self to integrate these energies into your energetic field now in order to help you align more fully with your divine life blueprint and soul purpose here on Earth.

18. Visualize the pure white light of the Holy Spirit and the golden ray of Christ surrounding you in a pure bubble of light. Repeat, "The Holy Spirit and the Christ Consciousness seal this healing with love and light." Repeat this 3 times.

19. Give thanks to your Angelic support team and your Higher Self.

20. Notice the feelings in your body.

21. Wiggle your fingers and toes.

22. Open your eyes and you are now fully awake.

23. I encourage you to now get out your journal and use this template if you feel guided:

    a. What did I see during this activation?

        i. What colors did I see?

        ii. What else did I see?

        iii. What do these colors and

visualizations mean?

b. What did I hear during this activation?

c. What did I feel during this activation?

d. What messages did I receive during this activation?

e. What did it feel like to connect with my Higher Self?

f. What did I learn from this activation?

CHAPTER 3: ANGEL NUMBERS

Numbers are a direct link to the Angelic realms and higher dimensions of reality. They serve as a gateway to help us connect with deeper truths and symbolisms that the universe and our spiritual support team are relaying to us constantly. Whenever you see double, triple, or even quadruple numbers in a sequence, this is a direct message from your Angels and serve as a "wake-up-call" to help you get motivated and get working on the next phase of your spiritual journey. Ever since I was attuned to reiki and started consciously connecting to my Angelic support team, numbers were and continue to be a direct connection to my Angels. Angels love to speak through numbers and now that this has been brought to your attention, your Angels will start reaching out to you in this way as well.

So let's talk about what specific Angelic numbers mean. I will discuss the main number sequences that I have worked with and shed light upon a portion of what these numbers may be trying to tell you. The following is channeled information from my Higher Self and my spiritual support team.

Angelic Sequences of Light:

11- Is a master number and is relaying the message to ground higher vibrational energies into your energetic field, by consciously connecting to your earth star chakra located anywhere from 6 to 18 inches below your feet. In doing so, you are able to bring in a higher vibration of light as you progress on your spiritual path.

22- Is a master number that resonates with abundance, joy, manifestation, and connecting with your Higher Self. This number is a call to connect with your Higher Self in all that you do, and INVITE in a greater sense of joy, enlightenment, and mastery into your life.

33- Resonates with the Christ Consciousness energy and helps you connect with the Master Jesus. Jesus opens his heart and pours deep love, wisdom, knowledge, and truth into your heart center whenever you see this number.

44- This number sequence resonates with connecting to your heart. This is a heart centered number and reminds you to get out of your head and

27

into your heart.

55- Is a direct link to Archangel Metatron and a higher calling to awaken to your soul path of ascension. This means you are being called to tune into Metatron's healing frequencies and ascension energies, to help support you and your divine mission daily.

66- Resonates with the cosmic law of creation. It represents divine will and exuberance as you recognize your innate worth with dignity and grace.

77- Is calling you to tap into the magical essence of the number 7. This helps connect each of your seven core chakras, while linking them to a greater vibration of light through the higher Angelic Realms of Light.

88- Represents divine abundance and divine flow. The universe is trying to get your attention to let you know that you are following divine guidance and your material needs will be satisfied as you continue listening to your intuitive guidance and nudges from Spirit.

99- Represents the ability to see things from a higher perspective. It is recognition that you are rising above challenges and are able to see things with "enlightened eyes", if you will allow yourself to do so.

101- Represents letting go and letting God in all areas of your life. It asks you to pray more and worry less. Call upon Spirit to help you safely move forward and ask for help with ANYTHING that you need help with at this time.

144- Ascended Masters are with you, shining their divine light and frequencies upon you at this time. They are helping you align with God's Divine will and connect with your higher purpose.

Keywords: Unity, grace, alignment, sacredness, perseverance, knowledge, truth, authenticity, integrity, and wisdom.

111- Your hard work is starting to pay off and your dedication to your spiritual path is being rewarded. Allow yourself to take confident action in the direction of your purpose. Initiate action steps towards reaching your Divine calling.

222- Hold on, your manifestations are right around the corner. Keep steady focus and don't let anything distract you. You will be pleasantly surprised with the blessings entering your life. Trust and have faith in Divine timing.

333- Connect to the Cosmic Christ Consciousness and invite in a greater level of service work into your heart center. Allow the Ascended Masters and cosmic beings of light to help support you in grounding a higher vibration of light into your energetic field and into the planet at this time. You are called upon to help ground higher light to help with the ascension process here on Earth. Keep your vibration high and allow miracles in.

444- Your Angels are knocking at your door to reassure you that they have heard your call for help! Allow this extra Angelic help to bless your life and the lives of others through the power of grace and gratitude. Be thankful for all the love entering your life at this very moment.

555- You are in a time of transition and the Angels assure you that these changes will bring about great blessings in your life. Allow yourself to connect with the legions of light and your Master Teachers at this time, to keep you aligned with your highest possible vision and outcome.

666- A call of cosmic harmony and balance. Allow everything to align in a magical way! Bring harmony and order to your life by staying determined and seeking help from trustworthy colleagues and family members. Listen, as the answer you are seeking will be relayed to you shortly.

777- This is a truly magical number that brings spiritual abundance and divine blessings to every area of your life. When you see this number sequence, you are completely surrounded and supported and it is reminding you that you are exactly where you need to be at exactly the right time. You are aligned with Spirit and Spirit is on your side! You have successfully brought every single area of your life into balance, which assures success in all your endeavors.

888- This number represents cosmic abundance. It reminds you to connect with Lord Ganesh, to bring in cosmic harmony and abundance into every area of your life. You are listening to higher guidance with ease and your manifestations will be appearing shortly. Your financial situation is about to be blessed and you will soon meet someone who can help support you and your future endeavors. Give gratitude as you are successfully "in the flow".

999- You are coming to completion with a certain task or area of your life. You are being called to higher service work. Embrace your higher calling and destiny, and tap into your spiritual essence through meditation to receive messages on your next step. Archangel Michael will guide you as you venture forward and begin the next phase of your sacred journey.

1010- Spiritual awakening is happening and you are safe as you take the next step on your journey.

Take this time to journal and record any "aha" moments and synchronicities that the Angels are sending you this week, which will provide greater insight, clarity, and direction upon your path.

1111- Is a gateway to higher dimensions of energy that can support you and your soul work at this time. This number sequences represents an 11th dimensional gateway of energy has opened up for you and is encouraging you to "anchor in" energy from your Higher Self as well as the galactic keys, codes and activations being offered to you now. Meditate on this without judgment and allow yourself to RECEIVE.

1212- You are completely in-sync with the universe and taking the correct steps to manifest your soul work here on Earth. Reward yourself, as you are co-creating beautiful work here on Earth.

1313- Connect with your inner wisdom and let your light shine. This number resonates with the Divine Feminine energies and archetypal energies such as Mother Mary, Quan Yin, Lady Portia, Mary Magdalene, Lakshmi, and more. Connect with these female Masters to deepen your spiritual growth and lead with enthusiasm and grace.

1414- Work with the Christ energy to radiate peace, love, and harmony to everyone on your path. Be the light that you wish to see in the world. Master Jesus is blessing you and your purpose at this very second. Take 3 deep breaths while focusing on your heart center. Allow his love to fill every cell in your body, purifying and uplifting your energy now.

1515- You are wise and you are being called to work with the higher spiritual realms, to bring in beautiful frequencies of energy through your crown chakra to help initiate others on their spiritual path. This number sequence shows up as part of your service work here on Earth. Consciously connect with your God like self and radiate peace, love, joy, and enlightenment to others now.

1616- Work on staying focused and balanced as you move forward. Heaven is working behind the scenes to help you; you just cannot see it yet. Let go and allow time to rest. Take action when you feel guided.

1717- Grace fills you with beautiful, serene, and uplifting energy. Know that you are being guided and that your new ideas and projects are divinely orchestrated. Have faith and take action accordingly.

1818- A reminder to connect with nature and Mother Earth for divine strength to help enrich every area of your life.

1919- Time to contemplate your next move. Look at all the options in front of you. Ask your Angelic support team to guide you in the direction of your highest path that is in alignment with God's Divine will. Notice any intuitive nudges or synchronistic events taking place at this time, as they are sure to point you in the right direction. Be patient and trust that you are fully supported.

1122- This is a call to tune-in and connect with your highest authentic soul purpose. State, "I AM ready to align with my Higher Self and download and upgrade higher frequencies of energy that fully support me and my highest possible calling now. I now give permission to release any old and worn out energies that no longer serve me and my purpose. I AM fully supported as I align with my highest divine blueprint. Amen!"

1234- This is a message that everything is in divine order and you are completely on track. Have confidence in yourself and be proud of who you are becoming.

"I AM that I AM… And things are manifesting beautifully…"

Channeled message from Saint Germain

CHAPTER 4: COLORS

Another area of our life that is truly magnificent is the healing effects of colors throughout our lives. Until it is brought to our conscious awareness, we do not fully grasp the beauty and significance that color brings into our body, mind, and spirit. Color is a direct channel to Spirit, and Spirit loves to communicate with us through the use of color! From what you wear, to what colors you use to decorate your home, how your office space is setup, to the color of your vehicle, the Universe is constantly relaying messages to us through the use of color.

Before we discuss this further, I want you to get out your Sacred Keys and Codes to Activate Your Higher Purpose journal, and allow yourself to write freely and without judgment. Please answer the following questions:

1. What does color represent to me at this time?

2. How does color currently affect my everyday life?

3. What color themes do I notice in my life?

4. What does my home "feel" like?

   a. What color themes do I notice in my home?

   b. Is there a correlation between how I feel at home and the color themes I notice within my home? If so, do I need to take inspired action to make my home space more comfortable and whole?

5. Notice what feelings and thoughts come up in regards to color and notice any areas of your life that are brought to your attention at this time. This is spirit's way of giving you direct messages regarding areas of your life that either are uplifting for you and/or areas that need some attention and change to help you be more fulfilled in your everyday life.

So why are colors important? Why would I want to start focusing my attention on the colors in my life? Well, there are many reasons. For instance, the colors that jump out to you and that you see repetitively throughout your day can represent various chakras. This indicates that you may need more of a certain color in your life to help you balance your chakratic system, in order to find more peace and equilibrium in your body, mind, and spirit. When your chakra column is in balance, there is a sense of harmony on both an energetic and physiological level.

Once you notice what colors seem to be dominant or playing out in your everyday life, you can then take inspired action, letting your Angels know that you received the message and that you now would like to work on healing, upgrading, and balancing the certain chakra that needs to be worked on. Please note that each day is completely different, thus what you may be working on one day may be completely different than what you were working on the day before. Conversely, you may start to notice themes and specific chakras that are in constant need of your attention, which may benefit from a reiki treatment and speaking with a specialist in the energetic field. With that said, we now need to look at what colors resonate with each chakra.

At this point in our lives, I find it necessary to explain the 12 chakra column that is being "reawakened" for many at this time. We have 7 basic chakras that we can think of as our "core" or our foundation. As we progress spiritually, we add in 5 more chakras that help us with further development on our evolutionary paths, and with soul expansion, as we become aware of the multidimensional nature of All That Is. We are experiencing rapid spiritual growth during this particular phase of the Ascension process, which is taking place on an individual and planetary level at this time.

If you would like, you may pause and grab your journal at this time. You may ask your Angelic

Helpers to help you go through each of the 12 chakras and tell you what color corresponds with each chakra. I have found that the chakra colors can resonate with different colors at different times, especially as spiritual growth and transformation is occurring. For the sake of simplicity, I will write down the 12 chakras with their corresponding colors that seem to be universal at this time, with the help of my Angelic support team.

1. **Earth Star Chakra**- Brown and black. Silver tints.

2. **Base Chakra**- Red.

3. **Sacral Chakra**- Pink with luminescent orange hues of light surrounding the pink.

4. **Navel Chakra**- Orange.

5. **Solar Plexus Chakra**- Yellow with tints of

green and gold.

6. **Heart Chakra**- Either pure white with pink hues and/or green.

7. **Throat Chakra**- Blue.

8. **Third-Eye Chakra**- Indigo and lavender.

9. **Crown Chakra**- Violet, white, and gold.

10. **Causal Chakra**- Pure white.

11. **Soul Star Chakra**- Baby blue and magenta

12. **Stellar Gateway Chakra**- Pure gold.

So let's say that you are driving down the street and you notice that one person is wearing a green jacket. You drive a little further and you notice a little dog with a green sweatshirt on. You go even further and there is an emerald green van right in front of you. You begin to realize and become aware that your Angels are trying to get your attention to focus on your heart center. By stating, "Okay Angels, I got it," you are giving thanks to your Angels for this message as you have now successfully detected and decoded part of the message that the Angels are sending you at this time. You may now want to ask, "Is there any other message in regards to my heart chakra that I need to know at this time?" You may hear, feel, know, and/or see a visual of further information that can help you decipher the message. They may be asking you to get out of your head and into your heart, or simply to choose love instead of fear, as these are both important qualities that can help your heart center stay in balance. Next, we will go through specific colors and the messages they may hold for you. I will be writing this list by tuning into my Angelic guidance and asking that my Angels help me detect and decode the specific information, keys, and codes that these various colors hold in regards to my specific readers. Thank you, Angels!

1. **Brown**- grounding and connecting with Earth. Take a couple minutes to find your center and imagine plugging into your earth star chakra at this time to gain support, strength, clarity, and inspiration from Mother Earth. Keyword: **BALANCE**.

2. **Black**- connect with the Divine Feminine aspects of yourself such as unconditional love, kindness, compassion, and empathy. This will allow you to see things more clearly. Seeing black is a sign to ground down higher frequencies from your higher self and consciously go into the inner depths of your

soul through meditation to help you connect with your inner wisdom and creativity. Keywords: **EARTH** and **DIVINE FEMININE.**

3. **Red**- ignites passion, creativity, safety, protection, and overcoming obstacles. Red brings a sense of warmth and strength to yourself and your projects. It also is a sign of abundance and complete financial support in all of your endeavors. Keywords: **PASSION and STRENGTH.**

4. **Pink-** resonates with unconditional love, joy, inner child, innocence, renewal, and profound faith. It also represents a higher level of compassion and connection. Keywords: **INNOCENCE and PURITY.**

5. **Orange-** relationships, joy, creativity, and self-

expression. Orange relates with finding the joy in all that you do and represents the need to express yourself creatively in life, which helps ignite your inner fire and divine spark that you hold within. Keyword: **JOY.**

6. **Yellow-** resonates with confidence, trust, strength, abundance, self-worth and integrity. Yellow brings a sense of joy and wonder, while helping you deepen your self-love and trust in the universe. Keyword: **DIGNITY.**

7. **Green-** abundance, prosperity, balancing giving/receiving, heart healing, nurturance, growth, expansion, and divine compassion. Seeing green asks you to live in your heart and connect with who you truly are on a soul level. Keywords: **TRUE SELF, ABUNDANCE, VOICE OF THE SOUL.**

8. **Blue-** resonates with truth, self-expression, honesty, and clear communication. Blue is reminding you to speak clearly and to also be a wonderful intuitive listener. Let your voice be heard and allow your true authentic self to shine! Keyword: **COMMUNICATION.**

9. **Indigo-** open up to your intuitive nature and allow yourself to see things clearly. You are becoming more aware of energy and your surroundings. Spiritual awakening is taking place and you are encouraged to consciously connect deeper with your Higher Self and spiritual nature, by meditating and learning more about spirituality, and what that means to you. Look for signs and synchronicities, as they are about to appear very strong for you at this time. Keywords: **INTUITION,**

INNER-KNOWING, and CLARITY.

10. **Violet-** resonates with a very high vibration of spirituality. Deep inner knowing, claircognizance, and unity. Violet is reminding you to deepen your connection to spirit and affirm: "I AM divinely connected and guided. I AM in alignment with my Higher Self and true authentic path. I AM a being of light and I AM ready to embrace my destiny and purpose." Violet resonates with the visionary and leader. Keywords: **DIVINITY, HIGHER SELF, and SPIRITUALITY.**

11. **White**- Higher Self alignment, purity, grace, and all-encompassing love. White holds the frequencies of purity and the keys and codes of your Higher Self and divine blueprint. Connect with the pure white energy of the Holy Spirit

to deepen your connection to All That Is and to embrace yourself fully on a soul level. White is all-inclusive and holds the vibrations of ALL colors, creating total balance and harmony within and without. As above, so below. Keywords: **PURITY and GRACE.**

12. **Light Blue-** resonates with compassion, lightness, and nurturance. Mother Mary steps down her all-encompassing love, truth, and wisdom through the light blue hues of energy. Keyword: **TRUTH.**

13. **Magenta**- is a color that brings in a higher spirituality. Deep inner wisdom can be found by connecting with the energy of magenta. Magenta connects you to your soul wisdom and helps you download and understand higher spiritual information, knowledge, and

truth. Keyword: **EXPANSION.**

14. **Gold-** gold is a magical energy that brings in renewal and rejuvenation, uplifting your entire body, mind, and spirit. It carries the higher light keys, codes, and activations of the higher dimensional blueprints for your destiny and purpose, and that of the entire planet. It helps to ground the Christ Consciousness energy and raise the vibrational frequency of all, transmuting all low vibrational energy to a higher and more loving form. Gold brings in great spiritual understanding and is the color of the Masters and illumined Beings of Light. Keywords: **SPIRITUAL, TRANSCENDENCE, RENEWAL, ILLUMINATION, and CHRIST CONSCIOUSNESS.**

15. **Diamond-** brings in a higher dimensional energy of purity and angelic light codes and activations. Diamond light frequencies allow great healing to take place and awakens our multidimensional energy blueprints, allowing greater understanding as we progress on our spiritual paths. It opens us up to new communication patterns, soul allies, and helps upgrade our healing frequencies and connection to spirit. Keywords: **MULTIDIMENSIONAL and INFINITY.**

Now that we have discussed what the specific colors mean, we will go through various color exercises to help you create peace, balance, and harmony in your everyday life.

Color is a natural healing remedy. By thinking about a certain color, we can invite in a certain level of healing that can help us on many different levels. What we will do in this exercise is focus upon certain colors to help build a bridge of light between Heaven and Earth. Notice the use of color to help with this exercise.

1. Find a quiet place to sit where you will be free from distraction.

2. Light a candle if you would like, dedicating it to the Holy Spirit.

3. Connect to the cosmic anchor points in the center of the bottom of both of your feet. Allow yourself to visualize two golden rays of light beaming down through the cosmic anchor points on your feet, into the center of Mother Earth.

4. Connect with the gigantic ball of pure, pink energy at the center of the Earth, as you

connect to the Heart of Gaia.

5. You are now grounded and connected to the Earth.

6. Imagine the pink energy is coming up through your feet, ankles, knees, hips, abdomen and heart center.

7. Now notice that the pink energy meets with a golden energy in your heart center.

8. Give permission to the golden rays of energy to connect your heart, throat, third-eye, crown, causal chakra (3 inches above your head), soul-star chakra (8 to 12 inches above your head), and stellar gateway chakra (2 feet above your head) now.

9. Allow the pure golden beam of energy to continue upwards into the higher spiritual dimensions to link directly with Heaven.

10. Imagine the golden energy merging with a pure white light now. Allow a spiraling gold and white light to funnel into your stellar gateway, soul star, causal, crown, third-eye, throat, heart center, solar plexus, navel, sacral, base, and earth star chakras.

11. You have now successfully connected a flow of energy to help bridge Heaven on Earth.

Now, as you are relaxed and completely balanced, we will conduct a simple color breathing exercise to balance your chakratic column.

1. Start taking nice deep breaths in through your nose and out through your mouth.

2. Call upon the pure white light of the Holy Spirit and your Angelic support team to be with you now.

3. State that you would like to build and

strengthen your Antahkarana (Pronounced: an-tah-kah-rana) bridge to pure source energy now. Your Antahkarana Bridge is a pure white tube of light that connects all of your chakras, running centrally down your body, connecting you to Mother Earth and extending all the way up to the Heavens, to allow for deeper spiritual connection.

4. Allow yourself to slowly start breathing in through your nose, pure white light. Allow yourself to visualize white light out in front of you, and give permission to the white light to enter in as you breathe in and fill every single cell of your being with it's pure, unconditional love.

5. Take 7 to 12 deep breaths, allowing the white light to fill your entire body completely. This

will cleanse, clear, and purify your entire energetic bodies almost immediately.

6. If you get distracted, this means that you need the specific vibrations that these colors have to offer. Continue for as long as you need, making sure that you find your balance.

7. Now, breathe in a pure, golden energy with the intention to balance your stellar gateway chakra. Complete 3 deeps breaths. Then state, "My stellar gateway chakra is now balanced and aligned."

8. Start breathing in a light blue and magenta energy in through your nose, and visualizing this energy entering every cell of your body. Continue for 3 breaths. Then state, "My soul star chakra is now fully balanced and aligned."

9. Next, breathe in a pure white light. Take 3

deep breaths. Then state, "My causal chakra is now fully balanced and aligned."

10. Breathe in a mixture of white, violet, and gold energy and call upon the gold, white, and violet flame. Breathe in this pure energy and allow it to swirl around and invigorate your body, mind, and spirit. Then state, "My crown chakra is now fully balanced and aligned."

11. Next you will breathe in indigo and lavender hues of light. Take 3 deep breaths. State, "My third eye chakra is now fully awake and balanced."

12. Then invite in a beautiful royal blue energy. Take 3 deep breaths. State, "My throat chakra is now being filled with the blue flame of Archangel Michael and I am finding it easier to speak my truth with strength and integrity."

13. Next, give permission to breathe in a beautiful pink and green energy into your heart center. Allow this light to radiate to every part of your body. Take 3 deep breaths, again, visualizing these colors entering in through your nose and out through your mouth. State, "My heart center is full of light and I am in total balance and harmony."

14. Invite yellow energy into your body now. Take 3 deep breaths, visualizing spiraling waves of yellow energy swirling around your abdomen now. State, "My solar plexus is balanced. I am strong. I am enough."

15. Start allowing an orange energy to enter your body and breathe this color all the way down into your tailbone. Take 3 deep breaths. State, "I am healthy and well. My navel chakra is

balanced and I invite healthy and harmonious relationships into my life."

16. Now call upon Lady Quan Yin and invite her orange and pink energy in through your mouth and down into your sacral chakra and every cell of your being. Take 3 deep breaths. State, "I am compassionate. I am kind. I am empathetic. I embrace my day with joy and enthusiasm. I have a mutual respect and deeper understanding for all. Today I respond with compassion. I am balanced."

17. Your next step will be to breathe in a beautiful red energy into your being. Take 3 deep breaths and focus in between your hips. State, "I am safe and protected. My base chakra is full of strength and vitality. I am full of perseverance and strength. I am supported in

all of my endeavors. My base chakra is now fully activated and balanced."

18. Lastly, breathe in an earthy brown and black energy down through your entire body and out through the soles of your feet. Take 3 deep breaths and feel the returning earthy energy being exhaled as you connect deeper with Mother Earth. State, "I am divinely guided in all that I do. Mother Earth supports my mission and destiny. I am full of courage and embrace my service work and higher calling with joy and enthusiasm. I am grounded, balanced, and well."

You have now successfully completed your first color breathing meditation and activation. You can see how powerful this simple exercise can be and it shows you a glimpse of the power that color holds.

This is a great way to start your day and a wonderful tool to add to your tool belt. Please take this time to get out your journal and write about your experience.

1. What colors could you see?

2. Did certain colors have specific sounds?

3. What did each color feel like?

4. Did certain colors evoke certain emotions?

5. Which colors did you feel drawn to?

6. What colors do you feel still need to be incorporated into your day?

7. What are some simple ways to incorporate these colors into your day today?

I encourage you to do this exercise as often as possible. The more that you practice this, the more comfortable you will get! You will begin to notice that certain colors start to call out to you and that you know which colors you may need to spend more time with each day and throughout the meditation.

If you feel like you need more than 3 breaths with each color, please take note of this and give yourself time to work with each individual color for as long as you need. Again, this will vary from day-to-day.

"Color is the music of the

soul."

Channeled message from

Saint Germain

CHAPTER 5: SOUND HEALING

Depending on our perception and our focus, everyone will perceive things a little bit differently. We may notice certain aromas that hold a special memory, be more inclined to see visual signs of the angelic guidance around us, or we may choose to busy ourselves completely, and become unaware of the beautiful energies that are all around us. One thing is certain though- we always have a choice on where we put our attention and focus.

One avenue that is a powerful healing tool is the power of sound and vibrations. No matter who we are, the sounds that we hear around us do influence our behaviors, thoughts, and actions. When we become aware of this, we can consciously choose to participate in the sound of our own heart. We can choose to find music and frequencies that support ourselves and our personal and spiritual growth. For instance, as I am writing this book, I am consciously choosing to play frequency 528 Hz, the frequency known as the "miracle healing frequency", also known as the frequency of LOVE. I was guided to play this music as I wrote, allowing this frequency to flood into and be absorbed into every page and every word of this book. In doing so, you will receive healing energy as you read each chapter of this book, that will support you and bring more unconditional love and joy into your life. That is my intention and I believe it will be so.

There is an ancient healing technique that talks about the Solfeggio Frequencies, and I encourage anyone who may be interested in sound healing and vibrational medicine to research this topic, as it is sure to spark an interest for you. I am no expert on this topic, but my Angels assured me that it is important to relay certain information to each and every one of you. The Solfeggio Frequencies can be used in healing, as each frequency resonates with certain healing responses, which are suggested to help one heal on the cellular level, evoking great healing in one's energetic bodies.

The Solfeggio Frequencies came to me early in my studies as a Reiki Master, to help me with some of my own personal healing that I needed to do, and I was shown a way to use this in my healing practices as well. I now choose to purposely use certain frequencies of music to help clients with their individual needs. Whether you, your family, or your clients are suffering from various ailments, need to let go of pain and worry, align with greater love, invite spiritual order and harmony into your lives, or all of the above, you can find sound frequencies to help promote healing and aid you in the process.

Another powerful sound tool is the use of chimes, gongs, singing bowls, etc. These items can be a valuable addition to add to your toolbox that can help not only yourself, but clients as well. For instance, I was gifted a pair of golden chimes from a friend of mine, and I love incorporating these into my healing sessions and to help balance my mind, body and spirit. Chimes are known to "call in the gods" before healing ceremonies and provide a direct link to the Angelic realms. Angels LOVE the sound of chimes and by ringing the chimes together, you automatically start attracting Angel Sonics into your life and your healing space. As you are working with your chimes, you may state, "Angels, please surround me with your beautiful Angel Sonics, and sing over me now." You will immediately feel uplifted, lighter, and feel more clear. Chimes also are a valuable tool to help cleanse, breakup, and disperse low vibrational energies. So, if you are conducting a healing session and you are having trouble clearing the energy in the client's chakras, you may grab your chimes and ring them over the chakras a few times, inviting in a deeper sense of healing. As soon as you are done, run your hands over the specific chakra (if appropriate) and notice how the energy has shifted. This is particularly useful for removing blockages that you feel unable to conquer. Energetic release then becomes possible. Whenever I use my chimes with clients, they report feeling more grounded, serene, and peaceful and truly enjoy this experience. Also, I like to use chimes at the end of a session to help seal the healing and to invite in greater peace and stillness. In order to do this, you can stand at the client's feet and state out loud, "let this first chime bring a greater sense of peace to your body, mind and spirit. Let this next chime bring in a greater sense of stillness, etc." I usually like to do 3 to 12 rings of the chimes, and allow the information from spirit to flow through, so every time I do this, it is different, dependent on the client's individual needs.

You can do this same sort of routine for yourself

by locating the chakra that is blocked and ringing the chimes in front of the chakra. Consciously breathe into this chakra as you focus on using the chimes. This should do the trick! If you really enjoy using the chimes, you can add these into your daily practice, allowing yourself to ring the chimes 3 times over each chakra. Once you have rung the chimes 3 times, state "My crown chakra is now balanced and awake". Then repeat and go to the next chakra. Allow yourself to do this with each of the 12 chakras (if you are healthy enough to raise your arms over your shoulders).

If you do not have physical chimes yet, I am going to walk you through a meditation to help you now.

1. Find a safe and comfortable place where you can be completely relaxed.

2. Call in Archangel Michael and your Angelic team of light to be with you now.

3. Call in the golden ray of Christ to surround you in a golden ball of energy.

4. Call in the Angels of Music and the Angels of Sound to uplift your vibration and to sing above you now and throughout your day.

5. Notice how your energy and mood change immediately as these Angels swoop in.

6. Ask the Angels to connect you with the song of your sacred heart.

7. Without judgment, allow yourself to be taken on a beautiful journey within, as you connect deeper with your sacred song.

8. Take as long as you need, knowing that you are guided, loved, and supported.

9. When you start to feel present, ask your Angels to place golden chimes in your aura, to disperse all low vibrational energies into a

higher and more loving form.

10. In doing so, know that you will be completely protected and supported.

11. You now are attracting greater Angelic support, peace, and harmony into every facet of your life.

12. Relax and breathe this energy in deeply, filling every cell of your body.

13. Smile and give thanks for the energy you just received.

14. Wiggle your fingers and toes and feel yourself fully present.

15. Open your eyes and continue on with your day.

I have had the pleasure of attending multiple singing bowl meditations by a wonderful sound healer, while participating in a healing expo in

Mankato, Minnesota. During these meditations, the instructor uses giant singing bowls and gongs to perform an hour and a half sound healing session. Throughout these sessions, I have found tremendous relief and healing and have almost gone into a trance-like state as we moved throughout the class. I found that I was able to completely let go, as it felt like I was transported to a completely different dimension. I bring this up because there is power in sound and it can really dislodge and shift your energy in a positive way, to enhance every single part of your being.

Please grab your journal and I want you to answer these questions now:

1. What kind of music do I listen to?

2. How does this music make me feel?

3. If you don't feel more inspired or uplifted

from the music you currently are listening to, are you willing to search for an alternative?

4. What instruments do you enjoy listening to?

5. Does this have any symbology?

6. What does music mean to you?

By answering these questions, you will learn a lot about yourself and your specific interests. It may help you gain clarity and insight on your likes and dislikes and you may notice things that you would like to change or add into your daily routine. This may help you find more meaning and fulfillment in your life.

Throughout my own personal experiences, I have learned that music can be a way to help lift you up when you need it the most. Several times, when I felt like I had hit rock bottom, a certain song would play on the radio or I would be guided to listen to a specific song. Low and behold, these songs turned out to be exactly what I needed, to help carry me forward and ignite the inner spark within me to rise above the darkness and reclaim my life as a sovereign being of light. I encourage you to really explore the music that you listen to and allow yourself to start paying more attention to the sounds around you.

BREATHE, BELIEVE, RECEIVE…

CHAPTER 6: SACRED SPACE

Whether you are a healer, psychic, or just a normal person trying to better your life, there are various ways that you can uplift the environment around you to create a healthier and happier atmosphere. Environmental health is extremely important, as many kids and adults are becoming more sensitive to the energetic grids, ley lines, and electromagnetics that emanate from technology, devices, and appliances. Our goal is to live as happy and healthy as possible. Keeping our space updated, pure, and clear is an essential part of keeping ourselves functioning properly as we reach towards our desired goals.

When we shift our attention and start focusing upon creating a sacred space in our external environment to deepen our spirituality, whether it be for healing, meditation, reading, or relaxing, we want to ensure that we feel safe and secure so we can get the most out of our experiences. By creating a safe place for yourself and others, you become a bridge of light, offering a safe place for those individuals to explore their spirituality on a deeper level. This is high level service work and a wonderful way to be the light in someone's world.

Creating a sacred space:

1. Fill the room with furniture that matches the vibe of the room you would like to create.

2. Choose colors that represent what you would like to create. For instance, my healing space is filled with blues (comfort, calming, truth, integrity, and soothing energy), gold (rejuvenation, recharging, higher spirituality, golden ray of Christ, inspiration, and divine connection), whites (purity & innocence), and browns (grounding, earth energy).

3. Pick out crystals that represent the energies that you would like to bring into your space. Rose quartz for unconditional love, quartz for healing on all levels, aqua aura to keep the vibration high in the room, citrine to attract warmth, prosperity and abundance, and so on.

4. Fill the space with specific objects that have

meaning. For example, I have Angels, Buddha, Quan Yin, spiritual accelerator images, lotus flowers, and other spiritual objects in my space, to invite in the beautiful energies of these objects and beings. This automatically uplifts the energy in the space and starts drawing in the appropriate frequencies of light to help create a healthy and loving space.

5. Place salt lamps in your space to keep the energy pure and clear. Salt lamps add tremendous value and energy to the space and help keep the environment pure and free from low vibrational energies. Placing three salt lamps in a triangular formation around the space invites in supreme protection. I use two salt lamps and one selenite tower to create

supreme protection in my space.

Space clearing for beginners:

Now that you have designed your space, let's talk a little bit about smudging. According to my personal definition, smudging is the act of cleansing a space by the use of various spiritual tools to create a happy and harmonious environment. We smudge objects, jewelry, crystals, rooms, and homes in order to clear out old and stuck energies and to invite more flow and abundance into the environment. By clearing a space, we allow ourselves to feel free from external influences by inviting in divine protection and various energies that can support us on our spiritual journeys.

Two of my personal favorite smudging tools are palo santo and sage. These are extremely potent and easy to use tools to help with cleansing any environment. You will need an abalone shell or something sacred or meaningful to you personally to keep these items in while you perform a space clearing. Once you have all the necessary tools, I recommend following these steps to clear your space.

1. Dedicate the sage, palo santo, or other cleansing tool to cleanse, clear, and purify the environment.

2. Light the palo santo and call in your Angels and guides to help cleanse the space. Blow out the flame, and allow the smoke to drift upwards as you go around the room.

3. Start at the door and go counter-clock wise around the room, holding the palo santo in your right hand.

4. Move your right hand in a figure eight

sequence (or any motion that resonates with you intuitively) over and over as you go around to each corner and along each wall. Say a simple prayer such as, "Angels, please cleanse, clear, and purify this space and bless this room with your beautiful Angel Sonics." Repeat.

5. Once you get around the entire room and back to the door, visually think of sealing the space with Divine love and light.

Once you have smudged the space, it is time to secure it with the power of the Archangels. This is a powerful tool that I have learned, that helps bring in powerful, yet peaceful energy, and lets you or anyone who enters know that they are safe and secure.

When invoking the Archangels, this is what I recommend:

1. Go to the corner closest to the door. Ask Archangel Raphael to be in this corner. Ask him to shine his beautiful emerald green energy upon your space and give him and his legions of healing Angels permission to bring in divine healing frequencies now.

2. Go counter-clock wise to the next corner. Ask Archangel Michael to be in this corner. Ask him to surround and protect your space with his shield and mighty sword and to guard the room from any low vibrational energy.

3. Go to the next corner invite Archangel Uriel to be at this corner. Ask Archangel Uriel to help ground higher frequencies of light into this space and to help with mental and emotional healing throughout the session and/or meditation.

4. Go to the last corner and ask Archangel Gabriel to be in this corner. Archangel Gabriel will wrap the room in pure divine love and light.

5. Then go to the center of the room and invoke Archangel Metatron. Ask Metatron to banish all evil and envision him on your ceiling, guarding above, and bringing in Heavenly energies to support you and your higher purpose.

6. Next, invite in Archangel Sandalphon to be below, helping ground higher energies into the Earth.

7. In doing so, you have now secured your space with the power of the Archangels. Know that your space will now bring peace to all who enter.

8. If you would like to take this one step further, you may ask your Guardian Angels to stand at your door, to constantly suck out all negativity and low vibrational energy, and to transmute this energy in the sacred flame of the Divine.

If you are certified in reiki and attuned to the reiki symbols, it is now time to go around to each corner, stating all the symbols that you are attuned to three times, with the intention of creating divine protection, and filling the space with unconditional love and light. Complete these steps for above and below as well. Then, state each reiki symbol three times in front of you and run your hands over your energetic field, creating a reiki bubble of light with each symbol. Each symbol will add another layer of protection to your being, ensuring that you are safe and secure as you do your spiritual work with yourself and others.

Lastly, envision a beautiful golden bubble of light above and a beautiful white bubble of light below your space. State, "God and the Holy Spirit surround this space three times in protection, three times in unconditional love, and three times in divine grace. Amen!" Your room is now pure and clear, and filled with divine energies. I recommend repeating these steps each and every time that you are going to be doing a healing or meditating yourself. The process should only take 5-10 minutes once you become comfortable with the steps.

Remember, music is an important tool to use as well. Bringing sacred music into your space will invite in higher frequencies of energies. Choose the specific music that feels right for your space and intend for the music to be absorbed into the space through the power of grace and gratitude.

"I AM the light, light, light.

Shining brightly each and

every day…"

Channeled Message from

Saint Francis of Assisi.

CHAPTER 7: ARCHANGELIC CLOAKS

When we think of the Archangels, we automatically connect with a powerful source of energy. The Archangels are extremely strong and vibrant beings of light that are here to support us on our soul's journey. They will help anyone, as long as they are pure in intention and are helping serve our Creator. They can help you align with higher frequencies, create miracles in your life and the lives of others, bring about peace and harmony, and provide you with creative solutions that are Heavenly sent. They can help you go with the flow, while maintaining a steady pace that suits you and your specific needs, all while deepening your service work here on Earth.

I am encouraged to share that each Archangel resonates with certain frequencies of energy and light, and they graciously share these energies with anyone who calls upon them and is ready to receive this light. With that said, I am going to explain a few of the Archangels and their specific cloaks of light that you may call upon for assistance in your everyday pursuits.

Archangel Michael- has a beautiful deep blue cloak that you can call upon and attune your energy with to help with protection, strength, courage, determination, motivation, and when you are in need of taking giant leaps forward. Whenever you feel a shift coming about in your life, be sure to call upon Archangel Michael's deep blue cloak of protection to be placed around your energetic body to serve as a shield to protect your from lower energies and to give you the strength that you need to move forward with ease.

Invocation: "I, (state your name), now call upon Archangel Michael to receive his mighty deep blue cloak of protection into my energetic field, now and always, to flawlessly protect me in all ways. I graciously accept this powerful gift and know that I will be protected today and all of my tomorrows. Amen." Repeat daily to build up strength and integration of this beautiful gift.

Archangel Gabriel- has a luminescent white cloak of purity. You may call upon Gabriel to share this cloak of purity with you to help purify your motives and intentions and to keep your energetic field clear of any lower vibrational energies throughout your day. This cloak will radiate pure white light into your aura, allowing you to feel inspired by grace, sharing this beautiful quality with all who you encounter.

Invocation: "Archangel Gabriel, please surround me as I receive your pure white cloak of purity into my energetic field now, to uplift and inspire me through divine grace. Please keep my thoughts and actions in alignment with my true purpose here on Earth, and allow me to feel your loving presence throughout my day. I graciously accept this beautiful gift and wear your cloak with the upmost respect. Thank you for guiding me throughout my day and inspiring me to do good in this world. Amen."

Archangel Metatron- has two beautiful cloaks that you can call upon to help uplift your energy and fill your energy field and life with Divine harmony and balance. The first cloak you can call upon, through divine will and intent, is Archangel Metatron's golden cloak of perfect harmony and divine wisdom. This energetic cloak will help to balance all of your 12 chakras while keeping them functioning at a 5th Dimensional frequency to help you with your own ascension process, and the ascension process of the Earth. His silver cloak will help bring divine balance into your energetic field, while amplifying the golden energy in your energetic field. This golden energy is bringing in a new sense of peace, balance, enlightenment, and harmony to every aspect of your being.

Invocation: "Archangel Metatron, please place your gold and silver cloaks of higher mastery and higher enlightenment around my body now. Please fill these cloaks with the qualities of strength, wisdom, clarity, purpose, knowledge, truth, protection, understanding, enlightenment, and self-mastery. I graciously accept these gifts and wear these cloaks with honor. Amen!"

Archangel Sandalphon- has a copper cloak of strength, courage, amplification, and grounding. This cloak is ideal for anyone who needs strength moving forward on their path and needs an energy boost. Sandalphon knows exactly what energy you need to connect with to create balance and focus in your life. Sandalphon is also in charge of the earth star chakra, so he can help you connect with Mother Earth to help ground your manifestations into your physical reality, always in divine timing, through grace and gratitude.

Invocation: "Archangel Sandalphon, please wrap me in your copper cloak of strength and courage to bestow upon me the qualities that I need to help create better balance in my life. Please allow this cloak to energize my body, mind, and spirit in an uplifting way. I graciously accept this gift as my heart is now full of joy. Amen!"

Archangel Raphael- has an emerald green cloak of healing that can be called upon whenever you or someone else is in need of healing. The emerald color and healing frequencies of Archangel Raphael are imbued in this cloak, allowing one to heal on a mental, emotional, physical, and spiritual level, always in alignment with God's Divine will.

Invocation: "Archangel Raphael, please surround me (or this situation) with your emerald green cloak of healing. I give myself permission to wear your emerald green cloak and receive the healing energy that it contains. Amen!"

Archangel Uriel- has a ruby cloak of strength and wisdom. This cloak can be called upon to help build confidence and self-esteem, while eliminating the effects of depression and anxiety. This cloak can remove self-limiting beliefs by replacing them with balanced awareness and fortitude. This is a powerful tool for the "underdog" and anyone who needs a spiritual boost and leg-up.

Invocation: "Archangel Uriel, I invoke your ruby cloak of strength and wisdom now. Please fill me with courage and boost my self-esteem while inspiring me to be more like you. Allow me to remain humble on my path and stay true to myself and my purpose. Amen!"

These Archangelic cloaks are powerful ascension tools that can be integrated into your energetic field to help assist you as you move forward. Just like anything else, the more that you practice connecting with these frequencies, the stronger and more capable you will feel.

I encourage you all to take out your journals now. Practice visualizing these Archangelic cloaks around you, by practicing each of the invocations above. Do each one individually and then pause and allow yourself to write in your journal:

1. What did you see?

2. What did you feel?

3. What did you hear?

4. What did you know?

5. Did this feel familiar or foreign?

6. What emotions did you notice?

.

"Simplify your life, allow

yourself to become

golden…"

Channeled message from

Archangel Metatron

8 ANGEL PRAYERS

I am a firm believer in the power of prayer. I believe that every positive thought, word, and deed that is done with pure intention, and from the heart, is energized with a beautiful ray of light that is sent out to help in the best possible way. Prayer is a direct connection to God and our Creator. Therefore, through prayer, we directly communicate with God and allow ourselves to build a relationship, just like any other relationship, from this connection. This connection is beautiful and wonderful, and I believe that the more attention you give to connecting with God, the stronger that connection can become. Think of building a relationship- it usually takes time, it takes commitment, and it takes love, honesty, compassion, and nonjudgment. Think of bestowing these qualities upon your relationship with our Creator, and allow your relationship to blossom in a way that is perfect for you at any given moment. When we connect with God, we feel safe, we feel secure, even just for a minute, allowing ourselves to fully trust that someone is listening and that someone is helping us through the challenges that seem unbearable. To trust that we are being heard, to trust that we are being helped, to trust that there is a greater plan, gives meaning and purpose to our lives. This is the foundation of faith-believing that we will be supported, we will be helped, and we will be heard. With faith, I truly believe that anything is possible. With that knowledge, I recognize myself as an infinite being of light. With that truth, miracles become a part of my everyday life. Through that wisdom, I am that I am.

I believe that we have unlimited support in the Angelic and spiritual realms to help assist us in every area of our lives. There is no task that is too big or small for the Angelic legions of light. By attuning ourselves to the Angelic realms and the divine help that is always available to us, we give permission for spirit to help us in our daily lives, and to help us accomplish that which we have come here to do. By knowing this, why wouldn't we ask for and allow help into our lives?

I am going to allow the Angels to work with my Higher Self to assist me in writing the exact prayers that can benefit my readers at exactly the time they need it. Since you are reading this chapter now, this is probably a good time to incorporate these prayers into your daily routine. If you need or want to modify or change a word here or there, please do so without hesitation, to help you align more fully with your true authentic path.

Angels of Wisdom:

"Angels of Wisdom please guide my actions and assure that I stay connected to my inner wisdom throughout my day. Help me act authentically and with purpose, as I work on deepening my connection to All That Is. Thank you."

Angels of Inspiration:

"Angels of Inspiration and divine grace, please watch over me today. Please fill every cell of my being with the pure white light of the Holy Spirit. Please assist me in tapping into my divine creativity and help inspire me to serve on a greater level. I am ready. Amen!"

Angels of Knowledge:

"Angels of Knowledge, please help me connect to my inner truth and help bring to me the dispensations of knowledge that support me and my spiritually based path. I am ready to receive. Amen!"

"Angels of Knowledge, I know that you are with me. Please guide me to the right people, places, resources, and opportunities that can further develop and awaken the innate knowledge that I hold within, always in divine right timing. Amen!"

Angels of Fire:

"Angels of Fire, please blaze your fiery energy upon my path to smooth my Ascension pathway and remove unneeded obstacles. Please bring a new sense of vibrancy, passion, and strength to all of my endeavors. Amen!"

Angels of Air:

"Angels of Air, please help me let go of the need to control and help me align with the flow of the universe. Please allow my life to line up and flow with dignity and grace. Amen!"

"Angels of Air please spread cosmic wisdom, knowledge, and truth upon me and my path now. Please spread the qualities of truth, enlightenment, and self-mastery everywhere I go today. Please send these qualities to uplift any areas in need today. I am blessed. Thank you!"

Angels of Water:

"Angels of Water please cleanse all aspects of my life and help me heal from any emotional pain and suffering. Please purify my thoughts, words, and deeds to allow greater miracles into my life. I connect with the power of water, and ask for pure ascension light to wash over me now. Amen!"

Angels of Earth:

"Angels of Earth, please help me stay grounded and balanced today. Please help me connect with Lady Gaia to deepen my connection and to assist me on the next phase of my spiritual journey. I am ready, I am ready, I am ready. Amen!"

Solar Angels:

"Solar Angels, please help me connect to the great central sun for illumination of spirit and personal growth. Please fill my aura with the golden energies of the sun. I invite warmth, creativity, wisdom, strength, and courage into my body now. I am now a focus of the great central sun, and I act with integrity today. Thank you!"

Lunar Angels:

"Lunar Angels, please bathe my being in lunar energies of the divine feminine. Help me connect to the sacred wisdom of the divine feminine, and help me build my divine feminine qualities of compassion, kindness, empathy, imagination, and intuition. I give thanks for the blessings I am about to receive. Amen!"

Angels of Animals:

"Angels of Animals, please bless our Earth's animals with beautiful light, to help them with all aspects of their soul's journey. Please ensure that they are watched over, protected, and treated fairly. I ask for extra love and support to be sent to the animals at this time. Amen!"

Angels of Creativity:

"Angels of Creativity, please fill my day with creative inspiration. Please bless all of my projects and endeavors with creativity and uplift my spirit to ensure the greatest outcome. Please guide me to express my creativity in healthy ways that benefits all. Amen!"

Angels of Abundance:

"Angels of Abundance, please bring an abundance of prosperity, wisdom, truth, resources, and healing into my life now. Please help me shift my attention and energy to embrace abundance consciousness now. Please work with my Higher Self to clear old patterns that are not in accordance with divine will. I give thanks in advance for the abundance entering my life, and I graciously accept all good things. Amen!"

Angels of Love:

"Angels of Love, please bring unconditional love and healing to all aspects of my life. Please help me accept unconditional love into my heart so I may experience a greater sense of connection with all things. Please attract healthy and happy relationships into my life now, which can support me and my spiritual growth at this time. Amen!"

Angels of Healing:

"Angels of Healing, please help me heal mentally, emotionally, physically, and spiritually in perfect and miraculous ways. I am open to receiving and I allow healing energy into my life now. I am whole. I am healing. I am healed. Amen!"

Angels of House Clearing:

"Angels of House Clearing, please cleanse my home of any stuck and stagnant energies. Please replace these energies with Angelic frequencies of love, support, warmth, comfort, and optimal health. Please help me keep my house pure and clear, and guide me to the best possible solutions. Amen!"

Angels of Finances:

"Angels of Finances, please help support me financially today and all of my tomorrows. Please help me be wise with my finances and make decisions from my heart. Please help me connect to my universal bank account and to my financial dispensations of light that can help me with my soul's purpose at this time. Help me live generously and ensure that I always have enough to live a happy and healthy life. Amen!"

Angels of Relationships:

"Angels of Relationships, please help me attract others who serve my highest good. Please help me have happy and harmonious relationships, and help me heal from any relationships that have caused my heart pain. I forgive people from my past, and welcome in new and positive relationships that better suit my needs at this time. I invite and give myself permission to experience more laughter, love, and comfort in all of my relationships. Thank you!"

Angels of Protection:

"Angels of Protection, please protect me and all that I do with the pure white light of the Holy Spirit. Please surround my life purpose and every facet of my life with the pure white light of the Holy Spirit and the golden ray of Christ. Continue to watch over me and shield me from any and all harsh energies, so I may be a beacon of light for others. Amen!"

Angels of Ascension:

"Angels of Ascension, please help me connect with my Ascension pathway, and lead the way forward. Please help me grow personally and spiritually as I set my intention to be of service on a greater level. Please help me connect with my sacred keys and codes to help assist me in all areas of my ascension pathway, helping me focus completely on divine love through loving service to the divine. Amen!"

Angels of Music:

"Angels of Music, please guide me to listen to music that resonates with me at this time. Please help uplift and inspire me and allow the frequencies of the music to heal my body, mind, and spirit. Amen!"

Angels of Grace:

"Angels of Grace, please fill me with your loving grace. Help me connect with the lightness and pureness of God's almighty serenity and peace. Let my soul find solitude in the divine grace that is being offered to me now. I am grateful. Amen!"

Angels of Writing:

"Angels of Writing please bless my projects and

help me journal and write about experiences that have helped me thus far. Please give me the courage to write down the sacredness that is inside of me in a beautiful and loving way. Please remove any obstacles that stand in my way, and help me remain in a state of gratitude as I write down my feelings. Amen!"

Angels of Spiritual Gifts:

"Angels of Spiritual Gifts, please help me channel my spiritual gifts and reclaim my power as a sovereign being of light. Please help me use my gifts only for the greatest and highest good of all, with respect and kindness for all living beings. Thank you for guiding me and teaching me more about my natural gifts and talents. Amen!"

Angels of Purpose:

"Angels of Purpose, please help me connect with my divine life blueprint and sacred purpose here on

Earth. Help me receive clarity and guidance on my sacred mission and purpose here on Earth. Help me remember who I am, and help things align in a beautiful way as I step into greater self-mastery and understanding. Amen!"

Angels of Meditation:

"Angels of Meditation, please deepen my ability to meditate and let go, allowing greater insight, clarity, and guidance to come through during my daily meditations. Please help me detect and decode the information that I am receiving. I give thanks in advance for all that I am receiving. Amen!"

Angels of Exercise:

"Angels of Exercise please help me safely and effectively commit to a workout routine that fits my specific goals and aspirations at this time. Please help me stay accountable and help me take the necessary action steps to move forward in a positive direction with my health. Please cheer me on and encourage me throughout my workout. Thank you!"

Angels of Nutrition:

"Angels of Nutrition, please help me to eat healthy and guide me to the foods that can keep my energy pure and clear, bringing a greater sense of peace and well-being to my body, mind, and spirit. Thank you for helping me change my relationship with food, and allowing the foods that I eat to nourish me on a soul level. Amen!"

Angels of Addiction:

"Angels of Addiction, please help me release and overcome any and all addictions that I am facing in my life at this time. Please help me love myself unconditionally and guide me to take steps in the right direction. I ask for you divine intervention in my

119

life to help me overcome any obstacles that stand in my way. Help me see clearly and see through the eyes of my Higher Self, allowing me to reclaim my innocence and joy. Amen!"

Angels of Joy:

"Angels of Joy, please be with me today to help bring laughter and joy into my life. Help me not take myself too seriously and help me remember the power of laughter. Please pave the way forward, inviting a greater sense of joy into every single area of my life. Please help me remember that I am on Earth to experience joy. Amen!"

Angels of Focus:

"Angels of Focus, please help me focus on the most important tasks at hand. Help me boost my concentration and help me complete projects and tasks with ease. Please eliminate any and all distractions that may stand in my way. Amen!"

Angels of Strength:

"Angels of Strength, please infuse my body, mind, and spirit with strength and courage. Please bestow upon me fortitude and determination to take positive steps in the right direction. Thank you for giving me strength in this time of need. Help me see any and all challenges as a way to grow, and give me the strength to overcome anything that stands in my way, through grace and gratitude. Amen!"

Angels of Divine Right Timing:

"Angels of Divine Right Timing, please ensure that I am ALWAYS in the right place at the right time. I invite divine synchronicity and divine miracles into my life now. Amen!"

Angels of Travel:

"Angels of Travel please keep me safe and secure

as I travel. Please guide me to places around this world where I can be of service and experience the greatest joy. Amen!"

Angels of Crystals:

"Angels of Crystals, please guide me to the best crystals that can support me and my day today. Please allow these crystals to bless me and my soul path. Amen!"

Christ Consciousness:

"I pray to the Christ Consciousness to wrap me in golden light, to help me stay true to myself and my authentic purpose, and to fill me with divine grace. I pray to deepen my connection with this powerful energy as I step into my power and serve humanity, and the Earth, on a greater level. Help me recognize the Christ light within me and allow me to share this light with all who I encounter today. Amen!"

Violet Flame:

"I now wish to connect with Archangel Zadkiel, the true Ascended Master Saint Germain, and the Violet Flame Angels to wrap me in the violet flame of transmutation and purification. I now ask for the violet flame to blaze, blaze, blaze through every cell of my body and energetic field, to transmute the energies of the old, in order for me to bring in the new. I give complete permission for this beautiful and sacred flame to raise my vibrational frequency, as I welcome in my mighty I AM presence and connect with God and the Holy Spirit on a deeper level. I recognize that this is a sacred gift, and I promise to use it with only the upmost integrity and honor, through our Lord Jesus Christ, Amen!"

"Within every person, there
is a spark of the Divine."

Channeled message from
Archangel Metatron

CHAPTER 9: A LAST WORD

Throughout this book, you have learned many different tools, ideas, concepts, and prayers that can assist you in furthering your development on your spiritual path. This book will help jump start your ascension process and help you connect deeper with your higher purpose and calling. I believe that each and every one of you have a sacred purpose here on Earth and that this book has guided you in connecting to your deeper wisdom, knowledge, and truth, and has spoken to you on a soul level. Whether you are conscious of it or not, you have taken the necessary steps to move forward, allowing you to embark upon a happier, healthier and more enriching life.

There is still much work to be done, but rest assured, we are heading in the right direction. I encourage you to continue to listen to your inner voice and connect each day with your Higher Self and your spiritual support team. Take the lessons, activities, and guidance provided to you in this book and please, reference it often as it is sure to point you in the right direction. A simple way to do this is to start your day by holding this book out in front of you, stating your intention to receive the information that is pertinent to you at this time, and then flip the book open to a random page and see what information is provided. It may just be what you need to hear today.

Furthermore, I encourage you to continue to learn, and continue to focus on divine love, whatever that shall mean to you. Work diligently towards reaching your goals and commit to those things that mean the most to you. If I have learned one thing, it is that commitment to our goals and passions will never lead us astray. When we have pure intentions and motives, we act from our hearts, and that automatically magnetizes all that we need directly into our lives.

Remember, give permission to become in greater alignment with God's Divine will, and then allow yourself to go with the flow and invite miracles into your everyday life. Journal about these experiences, as they will draw more miracles to you.

Lastly, express gratitude in advance for all the blessings coming into your life. Shout it out, "Angels,

God, the Holy Spirit, Divine Messenger Angels, I AM grateful for all the blessings coming into my life that I just can't see yet!" Let your voice be heard, let your presence be known, and be well.

Until next time,

Cody Cooper

CHAPTER 10: TERMINOLOGY

Antahkarana Bridge- this is a beautiful bridge/tube of pure white light that connects all of your chakras with pure source energy. This serves as a direct link to your Higher Self and All That Is.

Ascension- The process of raising your vibrational frequency and connecting to your most authentic self and soul purpose while focusing on divine love and divine service.

Angel Sonics- Angelic vibrations of light that uplift,

inspire, and purify everyone and everything that they touch.

Chakra- an energy wheel and power center existing in your etheric and physical body. Each chakra corresponds with specific anatomical, physiological, and spiritual functions in your energetic and physical bodies. When each chakra is balanced and aligned, harmony and balance exist in one's body, mind, and spirit.

Christ Consciousness- The pure state of enlightenment and self-mastery that allows one to connect fully with the infinite creative forces of the Universe and our Supreme Creator, through our Lord Jesus Christ. This is the embodiment of pure source light, God consciousness, and higher development. The golden ray of Christ fills you with the qualities of ascension, spiritual growth and acceleration, and spiritual attainment as a sovereign being of light. Recognizing and remembering your true Divine essence is KEY to connecting to the Christ Consciousness pool of energy.

Higher Self- Your true divine essence which is already whole, complete, and focused completely on divine love. This part of you is already completely healed in a spiritual sense.

Pure White Light of the Holy Spirit- Ascension tool to help purify your body, mind, and spirit. This tool can be used to enhance all of your projects and activities of daily life. The pure white light of the Holy Spirit can be called upon to protect you and your divine life mission and purpose each and every day. This can also be used to seal an energetic healing, ritual, or ceremony with the highest vibration of light that we can embody at this time.

Violet Flame- A spiritual tool gifted from the higher planes of existence that help transmute and transform lower energies to a higher form. Used for karmic balancing and is assisting the evolution of humanity and our planet at this time. Archangel Zadkiel and Ascended Master Saint Germain are in charge of this Ascension tool.

ABOUT THE AUTHOR

Cody was introduced to reiki and spiritually based healing in 2014, and was instantly intrigued by this sacred healing technique. He began seeking out resources to learn more about reiki and natural healing, which motivated him to become a Reiki Master in 2015. During Cody's first professional reiki session, he had a profound and miraculous experience. This reawakened many different spiritual gifts for Cody, which led him into his current role as a Spiritual Healer, Teacher, Author, Akashic Librarian, Psychic, and Divine Channel. Cody has a strong connection with Angels, Archangels, and Ascended Masters, and serves as a channel for these higher light beings. Cody also works with the Christ Consciousness energy to help others raise their vibrational frequency, allowing one to get into alignment with their divine life blueprint. Cody helps others recognize their true soul essence, and works as a guide to help others achieve their full potential.

You may also like:

Therapy for the Soul: An Intuitive's Guide to

Reaching Your Divine Potential

By: Cody Cooper

In this book, Cody explains various spiritual

tools and outlets that can be used to deepen your

connection to your own intuitive abilities and learn

various ways to bring peace and balance to your

own life and energetic bodies. This book offers

support for the sensitive, empathic, spiritual seeking

souls who are looking to raise their vibrational

frequency and commit to their spiritual growth and

awakening in this time of need.

Made in the USA
Lexington, KY
26 January 2018